# GOD IS AGAPE LOVE

## WILLIAM H. LEWIS III

Copyright © 2025 by William H. Lewis III
Los Angeles, California
All rights reserved
Printed and Bound in the United States of America

Published And Distributed By
OliWil Publishing
Los Angeles, California 90062
OliWilPublishing@gmail.com

Packaging/Consulting
Professional Publishing House
1425 W. Manchester Ave. Ste B
Los Angeles, California 90047
323-750-3592
Email: professionalpublishinghouse@yahoo.com
www.Professionalpublishinghouse.com

Cover design: TWA Solutions
First printing September 2025
978-1-7344901-2-1
10 9 8 7 6 5 4 3 2 1

No part of this book may be reproduced, stored in a retrieval system or transmitted in any form or by any means without the prior written permission of the publisher—except by a reviewer who may quote brief passages in a review to be printed in a newspaper, magazine or journal. For inquiries lewisbill1030@gmail.com

# ACKNOWLEDGMENTS

To my Lord and Savior Jesus Christ, thank you for everything. Lord Jesus, there is no me without you, there is no we without you, there is no us without you. Lord Jesus, you are everything, because everything is you. To Cynthia, my beautiful, strong, God-fearing, supportive, loving, caring, and nurturing wife. Thank you, babe, for having my back 1000% and for your unconditional love that makes me better each day. I love you with my whole heart.

To our three unique, beautiful, and beyond amazing children: Olivia, William, and Javier. The unconditional love, care, excitement, appreciation, humility, joy, and thankfulness that I have for the three of you is beyond words and measure. Always do your best and keep God first in your lives. I love you all unconditionally.

To Mom and Dad, I am humble, grateful, thankful, appreciative, and proud to call you my parents. Thank you for instilling in me everything necessary for me to be who and what I am today. I can never repay you for your countless sacrifices, nurturing spirits, and authenticity and sincerity. But most of all, thank you for introducing me to God. Mom, thank you for taking us to church and allowing us to grow in God, and to build our own relationships with God, and for your fervent prayers, I greatly appreciate you Mom beyond words and measure. Dad, thank you for being a true man of God and for inspiring me to be the best man of God I can be, I love you and Mom unconditionally.

To my brother Ced, I love you big bro. We have enjoyed some great times, but we have also endured some difficult times, but through it all, God was right there with us.

To my heart, my light, and my nurturer, my late, great, and one-of-a-kind sister, Ms. Natasha LaFrance Lewis. To say that I miss you Tash, would be the biggest understatement ever. I think of you morning, noon, and night. Thank you for everything Tash, and I will love you forever. God bless you always and forever.

To Dr. Rosie Milligan, an icon, trailblazer, legend, mentor, coach, mother figure, and just an all-around remarkable God-fearing woman of God. Thank you for believing in the gift that God put in me before the foundation of the world, the gift of writing. Dr. Milligan, thank you for giving me a platform to express my thoughts, feelings, and emotions. Most of all, thank you for giving me a platform to honor and glorify God. I greatly appreciate you beyond words and measure.

To my brother in Christ Jesus, Mr. Craig Releford. My good brother, I truly thank God for placing you in my life. You introduced me to the great Dr. Rosie Milligan, you helped me to realize my true purpose in life, and you have taught me so much through your vast knowledge, wisdom, intellect, spirit, uniqueness, and your love for thought and expression. I love you my brother in Christ Jesus and thank you for being a true friend.

And to my good brother in Christ and amazing friend, Mr. Lovell Williams. My good brother, thank you very much for your continued support, prayers, love, friendship, brotherhood, sincerity, humility, kindness, and thoughtfulness. God bless you and your beautiful family always. I truly thank God for your life and for placing you in my life so many years ago.

# ABOUT THE AUTHOR

William H. Lewis III was blessed by God with a gift for writing poetry meant to inspire, encourage, uplift, bless, and heal the wounds that life often inflicts upon us. He loves people and has dedicated his life to helping God's children become all that God created them to be. His purpose has been realized through a progressive, enlightening, spiritual, and life-changing relationship with God, for which he is truly thankful, honored, humbled, blessed, and grateful. William holds a Master's Degree in Counseling Psychology and a Pupil Personnel Services (PPS) Credential in School Counseling, with an Authorization in Child Welfare and Attendance. He proudly serves as an Academic Counselor at a middle school. William currently resides in Los Angeles with his beautiful wife and their three amazing children.

# TABLE OF CONTENTS

Introduction ................................................................. 1

Biblical Scriptures on Love ............................................... 3

God is Love .................................................................. 4

The Ultimate Sacrifice of Love ......................................... 5

God's Agape Love in Action ............................................. 6

God's Agape Love is Given to Everyone ........................... 8

The Four Types of Love in the Bible ................................. 9

What You are Put Here to Do ......................................... 10

The Law of Love ............................................................ 12

God is Omnipotent ........................................................ 15

Be Content .................................................................... 16

God is Everlasting .......................................................... 17

Poetic Expressions of Love ............................................. 18

Jesus' Agape Love .......................................................... 21

God Knows Your Heart .................................................. 22

The Good Samaratin ..................................................... 24

Inspirational Quotes ................................................26

Famous Quotes ........................................................29

Egg Shell ..................................................................31

Unexplainable ..........................................................32

Humility ..................................................................34

Even If I Don't Know You ......................................35

Scriptures on Humility and Service .........................38

We All Need Forgiveness .........................................41

Our Deepest Fear ....................................................45

God's Presence is the Present ..................................46

God First .................................................................48

Family and Sacrifice ................................................50

Love and Optimum Quotes ....................................53

Pentinent .................................................................55

Eternal Love ............................................................56

Reference .................................................................58

# INTRODUCTION

The epitome of God's Agape love for us was sending his only begotten son Jesus to die for sins. Without His courageous act of sacrifice and love, we would not have the abundant life that the Bible speaks about. And we love God, because He first loved us, and not just any type of love, like the love we often attach to things, but the highest form of love and charity. This love is shared between God and his children, reciprocity, and we show our true love for God by the way we treat one another.

And the Bible gives us guidance and clear examples of what true Agape love is:

1 Corinthians 13 4-8, *⁴Love is patient and kind; love does not envy or boast; it is not rrogant or rude. 5 It does not insist on its own way; it is not irritable or resentful; ⁶it does not rejoice at wrongdoing but rejoices with truth. ⁷Love bears all things, believes all things, hopes all things, endures all things. ⁸Love never ends. As for prophecies, they will cease; as for knowledge, it will pass away.*

Now more than ever, Agape love is crucial to our overall health and well-being, especially now, post-COVID-19. Truly we have all been impacted by COVID regardless of our status in life. Many people suffered monumental losses, which included loved ones that could never be replaced. And though things have improved, God's children are still suffering. So, my brothers and sisters, I want to encourage you to love one another from a Godly perspective, which is truly unconditional. And regardless of our gifts, talents, and desires to be influential, if it's not done with love, it's nothing.

In 1 Corinthians 13:1-3, it reads: *If I speak the tongues of men or angels, but do not have love, I am only a resounding gong or a clanging cymbal. [2]If I have the gift of prophecy and can fathom all mysteries and all knowledge, and if I have faith that can move mountains, but do not have love, I am nothing. [3]If I give all I possess to the poor and give over my body to hardship that I may boast, but do not have love, I gain nothing.*

# BIBLICAL SCRIPTURES ON LOVE

GOD IS AGAPE LOVE is relevant, thought-provoking, a spiritual awakening, timely, and hope for a brighter and better world. William H. Lewis III is extremely passionate, dedicated, and obedient to the will of God and the seed that He planted in him before the foundation of the world. GOD IS AGAPE LOVE truly emphasizes the true essence of God's love, compassion, humility, mercy, and grace which is the blueprint of God's expectation, desire, and will for all of his children, and how we treat one another.

This wonderful poetry book will inspire and encourage self-reflection, and a hunger and deeper desire for understanding, as well as sincerity regarding patience, empathy, awareness, consciousness, gratitude, and of course love. So, take a deep breath, get comfortable, and enjoy the Agape Love, lessons, and blessings of our Heavenly Father. To God be the glory, the honor, and the praise.

# GOD IS LOVE

**John 4: 7-14**

1. Beloved, let us love one another: for love is of God; and every one that loveth is born of God; and knoweth God.

2. He that loveth not knoweth not God; for God is love.

3. In this was manifested the love of God toward us, because God sent his only begotten Son into the world, that we might live through him.

4. Herein is love, not that we loved God, but that he loved us, and sent his Son to be the propitiation for our sins.

5. Beloved, if God so loved us, we ought also to love one another.

6. No man hath seen God at any time, if we love one another, God dwelleth in us, and his love is perfected in us.

7. Hereby know we that dwell in him, and he in us, because he hath given us his Spirit.

8. And we have seen and do testify that the Father sent his Son to be the Savior of the world.

# THE ULITIMATE SACRIFICE OF LOVE

**John 3:16-21**

1. For God so loved the world that he gave his only begotten Son, that whosoever believeth in Him should not perish, but have everlasting life.

2. For God sent not his Son into the world to condemn the world, but that the world through him might be saved.

3. He that believeth on him is not condemned: but he that believeth not is condemned already, because he hath not believed in the name of the only begotten Son of God.

4. And this is the condemnation, that light has come into the world, and men loved darkness rather than light because their deeds were evil.

5. For every one that doeth evil hateth the light, neither cometh to the light, lest his deeds should be reproved.

6. But he that doeth truth cometh to the light, that his deeds may be made manifest, that they are wrought in God.

# GOD'S AGAPE LOVE IN ACTION

## Romans 5:1-11

1. Therefore, since we have been justified through faith, we [a] have peace with God through our Lord Jesus Christ,

2. Through whom we have gained access by faith into this grace in which we now stand. And we[b] boast in the hope of the glory of God.

3. Not only so, but we[c] also glory in our sufferings, because we know that suffering produces perseverance;

4. Perseverance, character; and character, hope.

5. And hope does not put us to shame, because God's love has been poured out into our hearts through the Holy Spirit, who has been given to us.

6. You see, at just the right time, when we were still powerless, Christ died for the ungodly.

7. Very rarely will anyone die for a righteous person, though for a good person someone might possibly dare to die.

8. But God demonstrates his own love for us in this: While we were still sinners, Christ died for us.

9. Since we have now been justified by his blood, how much more shall we be saved from God's wrath through him!

10. For if, while we were God's enemies, we were reconciled to him through the death of his Son, how much more, having been reconciled, shall we be saved through his life!

11. Not only is this so, but we also boast in God through our Lord Jesus Christ, through whom we have now received reconciliation.

# GOD'S AGAPE LOVE IS GIVEN TO EVERYONE

While we were yet sinners, Jesus Christ died for us. Unmerited and undeserving. As children of God, it is extremely important and vital for us to reciprocate agape to our fellow brothers and sisters in Christ. Unselfish, unconditional, and putting others first.

*"Agape love is selfless love… The love God wants us to have isn't just an emotion but a conscious act of the will…a deliberate decision on our part to put others ahead of ourselves."*

–Billy Graham

# THE FOUR TYPES OF LOVE IN THE BIBLE

*Storge*—This Greek word describes family love, the affectionate bond that develops naturally between parents and children, and brothers and sisters.

*Phila*—The type of intimate love in the Bible that most Christians practice toward each other.

*Eros*—The Greek word for sensual or romantic love.

*Agape*—The highest of the four types of love in the Bible. Agape love is perfect, unconditional, sacrificial, and pure.

# WHAT YOU ARE PUT HERE TO DO

*"We must use our lives to make the world a better place to live, not just to acquire things. That is what we are put on this earth for."*

—Delores Huerta

### Agape Love One Another—John 15: 11-17

11. These things have I spoken unto you, that my joy might remain in you, and that your joy might be full.

12. This is my commandment, That ye love one another, as I have loved you.

13. Greater love hath no man than this, that a man lay down his life for his friends.

14. Ye are my friends, if you do whatsoever I command you.

15. Henceforth I call you not servants, for the servant knoweth not what his lord doeth: but I have called you friends; for all things that I have heard of my Father I have made known unto you.

16. Ye have not chosen me, but I have chosen you, and ordained you, that ye should go and bring forth fruit and that your fruit should remain: that whatsoever ye shall ask of the Father in my name, he may give it to you.

17. These things I command you, that ye love one another.

# THE LAW OF LOVE

"Whenever there are jars, wherever you are confronted with an opponent, conquer him with love. In a crude manner, I have worked it out in my life. That does not mean that all my difficulties are solved, I have found, however, that this law of love has answered as the law as the law of destruction has never done."

–Mahatma Gandhi

"We are made for loving, if we don't love, we will be like the plants without water."

–Bishop Desmond Tutu

"People must learn to hate, and if they can learn to hate, they can be taught to love, for love comes more naturally to the human heart than its opposite."

–Nelson Mandela

## God is Life-Genesis 2: 7

And the Lord God formed man of the dust of the ground, and breathed into his nostrils the breath of life; and man became a living soul.

## God is Omniscient ( All knowing) 1 John 3:20

For if our heart condemn us, God is greater than our heart, and knoweth all things

## God is Omnipresent (Present in all places at all times) Psalm 139: 7-14

7. Whither shall I go from thy spirit? Or whither shall I flee from thy presence?
8. If I ascend up into heaven, thou art there: If I make my bed in hell, behold, thou art there.
9. If I take the wings of the morning, and dwell in the uttermost parts of the sea;
10. Even there shall thy hand lead me, and thy right hand shall hold me.
11. If I say, Surely the darkness shall cover me; even the night shall be light about me.
12. Yea, the darkness hideth not from thee; but the night

shineth as the day: darkness and the light are both alike to thee.

13. For thou hast possessed my reins: thou hast covered me in my mother's womb.

14. I will praise thee; for I am fearfully and wonderfully made: marvelous are thy works; and that my soul knoweth right well.

# GOD IS OMNIPOTENT

**God is Omnipotent (Unlimited power) Psalm 147: 1-5**

1. Praise ye the Lord: for it is good to sing praises unto our God; for it is pleasant; and praise is comely.

2. The Lord doth build up Jerusalem: he gathered together the outcasts of Israel.

3. He healeth the broken in heart, and bindeth up their wounds.

4. He telleth the number of the stars; he calleth them all by their names

5. Great is our Lord, and of great power: his understanding is infinite

# BE CONTENT

**Be Content in Jesus Christ, regardless of the situation—Philippians 4:10-13**

10. But I rejoiced in the Lord greatly, that now at the last your care of me hath flourished again; wherein ye were also careful, but ye lacked opportunity.

11. Not that I speak in respect of want: for I have learned, in whatsoever state I am, therewith to be content.

12. I know both how to be abased, and I know how to abound: everywhere and in all things I am instructed both to be full and to be hungry, both to abound and to suffer need.

13. I can do all things through Christ which strengtheneth me.

# GOD IS EVERLASTING

## God is Everlasting—Isaiah 40:28-31

28. Hast thou not known? hast thou not heard, that the everlasting God, the Lord, the Creator Of the ends of the earth, fainteth not, neither is weary? there is no searching of his understanding.

29. He giveth power to the faint; and to them that have no might he increaseth strength.

30. Even the youths shall faint and be weary, and the young men shall utterly fall:

31. But they that wait upon the Lord shall renew their strength; they shall mount up with wings as eagles; they shall run, and not be weary; and they shall walk and not faint.

# POETIC EXPRESSIONS OF LOVE

## Plain Sight

Cruising through the streets in my luxury car

Not a care in the world and feeling like a star

Music bumping, AC on blast

Feeling calm and cool, but moving kind of fast

Out of the hood, I go

Into a whole different world full of rain and snow

Not literally

But figuratively

And all I see constantly

Is people living in poverty

No place to call home

No food to eat

No clothes to wear

No shoes on their feet

## *God is Agape Love*

No pep in their step

No pride in their stride

People walking around crying like somebody died

No life

No joy

No girl

No boy

No playing in the streets

No balls being thrown

Feel kind of scary like the Twilight Zone

This is not living

This is not life

This is hard times mixed with stress and strife

But no one seems to care about the other side of town

Where people don't smile, they only wear frowns

But how could this be

In the land of plenty

Greed and lies

Death and flies

Too much hate

Not enough love

*William H. Lewis, III*

We need the peace of God

Like a white pretty dove

But one day soon and not too much longer

The almighty God will make all his children stronger

In their faith

In the word

God is omniscient haven't you heard

He has all power in His Hands

But don't be surprised, because it's part of His plan

# JESUS' AGAPE LOVE

## Jesus Agape Love and Sacrifice—Revelation 1: 5-8

5. And from Jesus Christ, who is the faithful witness, and the first begotten of the dead, and the prince of the kings of the earth. Unto him that loved us and washed us from our sins in his own blood,

6. And hath made us kings and priests unto God and his Father; to him be glory and dominion for ever and ever, Amen.

7. Behold, he cometh with clouds; and every eye shall see him, and they also which pierced him: and all kindreds of the earth shall wail because of him. Even so, Amen.

8. I am Alpha and Omega, the beginning and the ending, saith the Lord, which is, and which was, and which is to come, the Almighty.

# GOD KNOWS YOUR HEART

"Let us not be satisfied with just giving money. Money is not enough. Money can be got. But they need your hearts to love them. So, spread your love everywhere you go."

–Mother Teresa

Agape love is a profound concern for the well-being of another, without any desire to control that other, to be thanked by that other, or to enjoy the process.

–Madeleine L'Engle

Agape doesn't love somebody because they're worthy. Agape makes them worthy by the strength and power of its love. Agape doesn't love somebody because they're beautiful. Agape loves in such a way that it makes them beautiful."

–Rob Bell

*God is Agape Love*

"Empathy is seeing with the eyes of another, listening with the ears of another, and feeling with the heart of another."

—Alfred Adler

# THE GOOD SAMARITAN

## The Good Samaritan—Luke 10: 25-37

25. And, behold, a certain lawyer stood up, and tempted him, saying, Master.

26. He said unto him, What is written in the law? how readest thou?

27. And he answering said thou shalt love the Lord thy God with all thy heart, and with all thy soul, and with all thy mind; and thy neighbor as Thyself.

28. And he said unto him, Thou hast answered right: this do and thou shall live.

29. But he, willing to justify himself, said unto Jesus, and who is my neighbor?

30. And Jesus answering said, A certain man went down from Jerusalem to Jericho, and fell among thieves, which stripped him of his raiment, and wounded him, and departed, leaving him half dead.

31. And by chance there came down a certain priest that way: and when he saw him, he passed by on the other side of the street.

32. And likewise a Levite, when he was at the place, came and looked on him; and passed by on the other side.

33. But a certain Samaritan, as he journeyed, came where he was: and when he saw him; he had compassion on him.

34. And went to him, and bound up his wounds, pouring in oil and wine, and set him on his own beast, and brought him to an inn, and took care of him.

35. And on the morrow when he departed, he took out two pence and gave them to the host, and said unto him, Take care of him, and whatsoever thou spendest More, when I come again, I will repay thee.

36. Which now of these three, thinkest thou, was neighbor unto him that fell among the thieves?

37. And he said, He that showed mercy on him. Then said Jesus unto him, Go, and do thou likewise.

# INSPIRATIONAL QUOTES

"Only a life lived for others is a life worthwhile."

–Albert Einstein

"Love and compassion are necessities, not luxuries, without them humanity cannot survive."

–Dalai Lama

"We all die. The goal isn't to live forever. The Goal is to create somethign that will."

–Chuck Palahniuk

"Our death is not an end if we can live on in our children and the younger generation. For they are us, our bodies are only wilted leaves on the tree of life."

–Albert Einstein

## Inspirational quotes by the great John Wooden

"Talent is God given. Be humble. Fame is man-given. Be grateful. Conceit is self-given. Be careful."

"If you're not making mistakes, then you're not doing anything. I'm positive that a doer makes mistakes."

"It's the little details that are vital. Little things make big things happen."

"Be true to yourself, help others, make each day your masterpiece, make friendship a fine art, drink deeply from good books—especially the Bible, build a shelter against a rainy day, give thanks for your blessings and pray for guidance every day."

"Success is peace of mind which is a direct result of self-satisfaction in knowing you did your best to become the best you are capable of becoming."

"The most important thing in the world is family and love."

"The greatness of a community is most accurately measured by the compassionate actions of its members, a heart of grace, and a soul generated by love."

–Coretta Scott King

"More smiling, less worrying. More compassion, less judgment. More blessed, less stressed. More love, less hate."

-Roy T. Bennett

"Compassion is not a relationship between the Healer and the Wounded. It's a Relationship Between Equals. Only When We Know Our Own. Only when we know our own darkness well can we be present with the darkness of others. Compassion becomes real when we recognize our shared humanity."

–Pema Chödrön

# FAMOUS QUOTES

"Nobody cares how much you know until they know how much you care."

–Theodore Roosevelt

"People will forget what you said, people will forget what you did, but people will never forget how you made them feel."

–Dr. Maya Angelou

# EGG SHELL

Misunderstood most of my life
Lied on
Lied to
Abused
Disrespected and called bad names
Rejected by most
Taken advantage of
Never felt true love
Only conditional love
I would rather have no love at all
I'm hard on the outside
I'm tough on the outside
I'm mean on the outside
I yell on the outside
I scream on the outside
I use bad language on the outside
I cry on the inside
I cry deeply on the interior
There have been times where I had tears, for breakfast, lunch and dinner
This is not living
It's difficult to explain
I pray

## God is Agape Love

I talk to God
God listens to me
I heard somewhere that God will never leave nor forsake me
God is my only hope
I have no family
I have no friends
I have mentors
I have no confidants
But I have God

To all of my brothers and sisters, please know that you are never alone as long as you have God in your heart and spirit
Lean on God at all times
Even when things are going well, because life is so unpredictable

# UNEXPLAINABLE

Deep-rooted and difficult to express
I've tried and tried but it turns into a mess
Crying uncontrollably
Needing someone to comfort me
I can't go on like this
But I'm not in the mood for a hug or even a kiss
Feeling numb and in disbelief
Unfortunately, we know it all too well, that thing they call grief
When was it created and why
No answer though, just deep sorrow when someone dies
Never to be seen again on this side of the dirt
No longer suffering, but the loss still hurts
Life is so short
Give love and show
Because we never know when our time will come to be on the front row
And I have to admit it's rough
And extremely tough
Soon as I walked in and saw the white casket, that was enough
But God gave me the strength to carry on

*God is Agape Love*

Because God is omnipotent and sits on a throne
So I give God the glory, the honor, and the praise, because He is the Prince of peace, which helps me get through those dark and difficult days

# HUMILITY

"Pride is concerned with who is right.
Humility is concerned with what is right."

–Ezra T. Benson

# EVEN IF I DON'T KNOW YOU

If I see you digging through trash cans, my heart is broken, my spirit is crushed

How can it not

I'm no different than you

If you cut me, I bleed

If I'm sleepy, I need rest

If I'm hungry, I need nourishment

I will not live forever, for one day I will transition out of this world just like you

Let's not pretend

Let's not be so focused on our goals and dreams that we forget about the people that are struggling in our presence and around the world

Thank God for that warm bed

Many are sleeping on the streets with the rats, roaches, and the overwhelming chill of night

Many are greeted with disdain and disrespect

Many are humiliated and embarrassed

It's beyond pouring salt on the wound

It's an insult

It's unacceptable

It's shameful

We all belong to God

God loves you

Jesus did not die on the cross for His children to look down on one another

Lift up your brother

Lift up your sister

Who cares about your mansions

## God is Agape Love

Who cares about your car collection

Who cares about your 100 pairs of shoes

Who cares about your 50 purses

Who cares about your name brand whatever

In this age of COVID-19, people are struggling more than ever

Can we please pay more attention

Can we please show more love

Can we please show more empathy

Can we please show more compassion

Can we please let God's children know that we care about them

Please

Please

Please

God is watching

God knows our hearts

# SCRIPTURES ON HUMILITY AND SERVICE

**The Ultimate display of humility and service: Jesus washes His disciples' feet–John 13:1-20**

1. Now before the feast of the passover, when Jesus knew that his hour was come that he should depart out of this world unto the Father, having loved his own which were in the world, he loved them unto the end.

2. And supper being ended, the devil having now put into the heart of Judas Iscariot, Simon's son, to betray him;

3. Jesus knowing that the Father had given all things into his hands, and that he was come from God, and went to God;

4. He riseth from supper, and laid aside his garments; and took a towel, and girded himself.

5. After that he poureth water into a bason, and began to wash the disciples' feet, and to wipe them with the towel wherewith he was girded.

6. Then cometh he to Simon Peter: and Peter saith unto him, Lord, dost thou wash my feet?

7. Jesus answered and said unto him, What I do thou knowest not now; but thou shalt know hereafter.

8. Peter saith unto him, Thou shalt never wash my feet. Jesus answered him, If I wash thee not, thou hast no part with me.

9. Simon Peter saith unto him, Lord, not my feet only, but also my hands and my head.

10. Jesus saith to him, He that is washed needeth not say to wash his feet, but is clean every whit: and ye are clean, but not all.

11. For he knew who should betray him; therefore said he, Ye are not all clean.

12. So after he had washed their feet, and had taken his garments, and was set down again, he said unto them, Know ye what I have done to you?

13. Ye call me Master and Lord: and ye say well; for so I am.

14. If I then, your Lord and Master, have washed your feet; ye also ought to wash one another's feet.

15. For I have given you an example, that ye should do as I have done to you.

16. Verily, verily, I say unto you, The servant is not greater than his lord; neither he that is sent greater than he that sent him.

17. If ye know these things, happy are ye if ye do them.

18. I speak not of you all: I know whom I have chosen: but that the scripture may be fulfilled, He that eateth bread with me hath lifted up his heel against me.

19. Now I tell you before it come, that, when it is come to pass, ye may believe that I am he.

20. Verily, verily, I say unto you, He that receiveth whomsoever I send receiveth me; and he that receiveth me receiveth him that sent me.

# WE ALL NEED FORGIVENESS

My brothers and sisters, with so much disease, destruction, violence, malice, and mayhem in our world, it would be wise to humble ourselves, pray, seek God, and ask for forgiveness

**2 Chronicles 7: 1-22**

1. Now when Solomon had made an end of praying, the fire came down from heaven, and consumed the burnt offering and the sacrifices; and the glory of the Lord filled the house.

2. And the priests could not enter into the house of the Lord, because the glory of the Lord had filled the Lord's house.

3. And when all the children of Israel saw how the fire came down, and the glory of the Lord upon the house, they bowed themselves with their faces to the ground upon the pavement, and worshipped, and praised the Lord, saying, For he is good; for his mercy endureth for ever.

4. Then the king and all the people offered sacrifices before the Lord.

5. And king Solomon offered a sacrifice of twenty and two thousand oxen, and an hundred and twenty thousand sheep: so the king and all the people dedicated the house of God.

6. And the priests waited on their offices: the Levites also with instruments of musick of the Lord, which David the king had made to praise the Lord, because his mercy endureth for ever, when David praised by their ministry; and the priests sounded trumpets before them, and all Israel stood.

7. Moreover Solomon hallowed the middle of the court that was before the house of the Lord: for there he offered burnt offerings, and the fat of the peace offerings, because the brasen altar which Solomon had made was not able to receive the burnt offerings, and the meat offerings, and the fat.

8. Also at the same time Solomon kept the feast seven days, and all Israel with him, a very great congregation, from the entering in of Hamath unto the river of Egypt.

9. And in the eighth day they made a solemn assembly: for they kept the dedication of the altar seven days, and the feast seven days.

10. And on the three and twentieth day of the seventh month he sent the people away into their tents, glad and merry

in heart for the goodness that the Lord had shewed unto David, and to Solomon, and to Israel his people.

11. Thus Solomon finished the house of the Lord, and the king's house: and all that came into Solomon's heart to make in the house of the Lord, and in his own house, he prosperously effected.

12. And the Lord appeared to Solomon by night, and said unto him, I have heard thy prayer, and have chosen this place to myself for an house of sacrifice.

13. If I shut up heaven that there be no rain, or if I command the locusts to devour the land, or if I send pestilence among my people;

14. If my people, which are called by my name, shall humble themselves, and pray, and seek my face, and turn from their wicked ways; then will I hear from heaven, and will forgive their sin, and will heal their land.

15. Now mine eyes shall be open, and mine ears attent unto the prayer that is made in this place.

16. For now have I chosen and sanctified this house, that my name may be there for ever: and mine eyes and mine heart shall be there perpetually.

17. And as for thee, if thou wilt walk before me, as David thy father walked, and do according to all that I have

commanded thee, and shalt observe my statutes and my judgments;

18. Then will I stablish the throne of thy kingdom, according as I have covenanted with David thy father, saying, There shall not fail thee a man to be ruler in Israel.

19. But if ye turn away, and forsake my statutes and my commandments, which I have set before you, and shall go and serve other gods, and worship them;

20. Then will I pluck them up by the roots out of my land which I have given them; and this house, which I have sanctified for my name, will I cast out of my sight, and will make it to be a proverb and a byword among all nations.

21. And this house, which is high, shall be an astonishment to every one that passeth by it; so that he shall say, Why hath the Lord done thus unto this land, and unto this house?

22. And it shall be answered, Because they forsook the Lord God of their fathers, which brought them forth out of the land of Egypt, and laid hold on other gods, and worshipped them, and served them: therefore hath he brought all this evil upon them.

# OUR DEEPEST FEAR

"Our deepest fear is not that we are inadequate.

Our deepest fear is that we are powerful beyond measure.

It is our light, not our darkness that most frightens us.

We ask ourselves, 'Who am I to be brilliant, gorgeous, talented, fabulous?'

Actually, who are you not to be? You are a child of God;

Your playing small doesn't serve the world."

–Marianne Williamson

# GOD'S PRESENCE IS THE PRESENT

It's not what you've been through, but what He brought you through

As we know, life is full of challenges, trials, and tribulations

Sickness, depression, anxiety, stress, sleep deprivation

Sadness, grief, pain, betrayal, poverty, and everything in between

But no matter what we have to endure, God is with us always and forever

God is dependable

God is reliable

God is immutable

God is everlasting

What a great joy and pleasureto know that God is able

And we often talk about what we've been through

And what we're still going through

## God is Agape Love

But fret not, because God is with us

We only learn and grow through the challenges thatwe suffer through

Jesus was crucified

Jesus was nailed to a cross

Jesus suffered

Jesus experienced life as a human being

Jesus experienced the unimaginable

Jesus will always be there to catch us when we fall

God's agape love is fail proof

Amen and Amen

# GOD FIRST

God first

God is everything because everything is God

God is the King of Kings

God is the Lord of Lords

God is Alpha and Omega

God is the beginning and the end

God doesn't need much to make plenty

Case in point, the two fish and five loaves of bread

Jesus looking up to heaven gave thanks and broke them

They all ate and was satisfied, leaving twelve baskets full of broken pieces that were leftover

When we seek God and put Him first, He will always bless us in abundance

God will never give us just enough, but more than enough

When God blesses His children, there will be leftovers and overflow

*God is Agape Love*

But we don't serve God for things, but for a relationship

And though God is the ultimate provider, He's so much more

Seek God daily

Pray everyday

Love your brothers and sisters unconditionally

Give cheerfully

Treat others the way you want to be treated

Forgive and give it to God

# FAMILY AND SACRIFICE

"This is part of what a family is about, not just love.

It's knowing that your family will be there watching out for you.

Nothing else will give you that.

Not money.

Not fame.

Not work."

–Mitch Albom

"Families are the compass that guides us.

They are the inspiration to reach great heights, and our comfort when we occasionally falter."

–Brad Henry

"You must remember, family is often born of blood, but it doesn't depend on blood.

Nor is it exclusive of friendship.

Family members can be your best friends, you know.

And best friends, whether or not they are related to you, can be your family."

–Trenton Lee Stewart

"Great achievement is usually born of great sacrifice, and is never the results of selfishness."

–Napoleon Hill

"Presumption should never make us neglect that which appears easy to us, nor despair make us lose courage at the sight of difficulties."

–Benjamin Banneker

"The important thing is this: to be able, at any moment, to sacrifice what we are for what we could become."

–Maharishi Mahesh Yogi

"The good and the great are only separated by their willingness to sacrifice."

–Kareem Abdul-Jabbar

"As we Give, we find that sacrifice brings forth the Blessings of heaven, and in the end, we learn it was no SACRIFICE at all."

–Spencer W. Kimball

# LOVE AND OPTIMISM QUOTES

"Love is the only force capable of transforming an enemy into a friend"

- Dr. Martin Luther King Jr.

"Love is a net that catches hearts like fish."

–Muhammad Ali

"Love and compassion are necessities, not luxuries. Without them, humanity cannot survive."

–Dalai Lama

"No one is born hating another person because of the color of his skin, or his background, or his religion. People must learn to hate, and if they can learn to hate, they can be taught to love, for love comes naturally to the human heart than its opposite."

–Nelson Mandela

"We need more light about each other. Light creates understanding, understanding creates love, love creates patience, and patience creates unity."

–Malcolm X

"Spread love everywhere you go. Let no one ever come to you without leaving happier."

–Mother Teresa

"We cannot change the past, but we can change our attitude toward it. Uproot guilt and plant forgiveness. Tear out arrogance and seed humility. Exchange love for hate thereby making the present comfortable and the future promising."

–Maya Angelou

# PENTINENT

No one is without sin

Not me, not you, or even your best friend

God knows your heart

Humility and kindness is a great place to start

The world can be cruel and challenging no doubt

But expressing sorrow and showing mercy is what I am talking about

And no, it's not easy

It takes courage and love

Pray for God's guidance from heaven up above

Just like the thief on the cross

Jesus did not think twice

I tell you the truth, today you will be with me in paradise

So forgive and be forgiven

And thank God for the life you're currently living

# ETERNAL LOVE

## The Eternal Love of God (Luke 23: 32-43)

32. And there were also two other, malefactors, led with him to be put to death.

33. And when they were come to the place, which is called Calvary, there they crucified him, and the malefactors, one on the right hand, and the other on the left.

34. Then said Jesus, Father, forgive them; for they know not what they do. And they parted his raiment, and cast lots.

35. And the people stood beholding. And the rulers also with them derided him, saying, He saved others; let him save himself, if he be Christ, the chosen of God.

36. And the soldiers also mocked him, coming to him, and offering him vinegar,

37. And saying, If thou be the king of the Jews, save thyself.

38. And a superscription also was written over him in letters of Greek, and Latin, and Hebrew, This Is The King Of The Jews.

39. And one of the malefactors which were hanged railed on him, saying, If thou be Christ, save thyself and us.

40. But the other answering rebuked him, saying, Dost not thou fear God, seeing thou art in the same condemnation?

41. And we indeed justly; for we receive the due reward of our deeds: but this man hath done nothing amiss.

42. And he said unto Jesus, Lord, remember me when thou comest into thy kingdom.

43. And Jesus said unto him, Verily I say unto thee, Today shalt thou be with me in paradise.

# REFERENCE

Zava, J (2020, May 11). 4 Types of Love in the Bible. https//www.learnreligions.com

www.ingramcontent.com/pod-product-compliance
Lightning Source LLC
Chambersburg PA
CBHW030559080526
44585CB00012B/426